Superlatives.

Superlatives.

The Superlatist

SHORT BOOKS

Published in 2012 by Short Books

Short Books
3A Exmouth House
Pine Street
EC1R 0JH

10 9 8 7 6 5 4 3 2 1

Copyright ©
The Superlatist 2012

Design: Georgia Vaux

A CIP catalogue record for this book
is available from the British Library.

ISBN 978-1-78072-110-1

Printed in China by Hung Hing

Contents.

Introduction.

My mother always told me never to exaggerate. My response was normally to scream "You're worse than Hitler" and burst into tears and storm off to my room, which took some time as I was about twenty by this point and lived several miles away.

I screamed it out the window of the top deck of the bus as I passed my mum's house back then, and I'll say it again now: there's nothing wrong with exaggeration. So what if exaggerating is a bit like lying? It helps us to tell a story. It helps us to find the humour in everyday life, even when things really don't seem that funny. It elevates the banal into something new and exciting and relevant. In the right hands, exaggeration can even help people to see the truth. The fact that I've used it for none of these things, and instead used it to take pictures of dog turds that look a bit like Charles DeGaulle, is beside the point.

So here it is – a collection of the best cameraphone photos from my blog "Superlatives". I hope you enjoy briefly looking at them and immediately putting them back down as much as I have enjoyed the last five years trudging the streets of London day and night, looking for something vaguely remarkable.

Had my mother known then that my uncanny ability to exaggerate things would result in this very book, who knows what she might have said? To be honest she probably would have kept her fucking mouth shut.

Yours,

The Superlatist

World's Worst Directions.

World's Least Subtle
Money Laundering Operation.

World's Most Heartbreaking Charity Shop Find.

World's Most
Forlorn Truck.

World's Sexiest Protagonist.

World's Single Most Confusing Image.

World's Least Necessary Path.

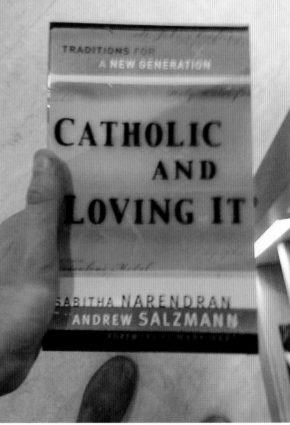

World's Biggest Lie.

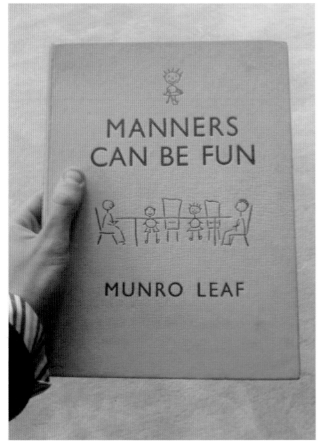

World's Best Marketing Campaign.

World's Most Sarcastic Job Ad.

symptoms such as radiating pain or numbness, or difficulties with bowel or bladder functions

• if you are more than three months pregnant

Basic Relaxation Pose

Props
• standard bed blanket

Optional Props
• eyebag
• long roll (towel or bolster)
• blanket (yellow or grey tones)
• extra blanket for warmth
• clock or timer

As explained in chapter 4, this pose is the heart of restorative practice. Relaxing completely, even if it is only for 5 minutes, is one of the most important skills you can acquire. When you have learned to relax whenever and wherever you need to, you can use this skill in a variety of situations to reduce stress and its accompanying fatigue.

FIGURE 6-1
Basic Relaxation Pose

Setting Up, Being There, and Coming Back. Refer to page 25 for full instructions. Practice Basic Relaxation Pose for 7 minutes.

Benefits. All the physiological measures of stress are reduced by a period of deep relaxation. Fatigue is diminished and life is just easier to handle when you are more relaxed.

Cautions.
• If you are more than three months pregnant, practice Side-LYING Relaxation Pose (see chapter 13).

Desk Forward Bend

I remember how restful it was during my school days to lean forward and rest my head and folded arms on my desk. Try this pose at your desk or in the lunchroom at work or school.

Props
• desk or table
• chair

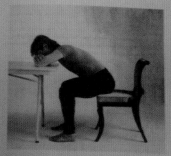

FIGURE 6-2
Desk Forward Bend

Setting Up. Place your chair (without rollers) near your desk so that you can easily lean forward. Sit at the edge of the chair seat, with your feet flat on the floor. Lean forward and place your folded arms on the desk, so your feet securely supported. Rest your forehead on your arms. Tip your chin slightly toward your chest. Close your eyes.

Being There. Breathe slowly and deeply for the first few breaths, then resume normal breathing. Let the desk support your arms, your head, and your cares. Let the next few minutes of relaxation fill you.

Coming Back. Practice Desk Forward Bend for 5 minutes. To come up, unfold your arms as you lift your head. Inhale, and press your hands onto the desk to help you return to sitting. Sit in your chair for

World's Laziest Yoga.

World's Bleakest Poster.

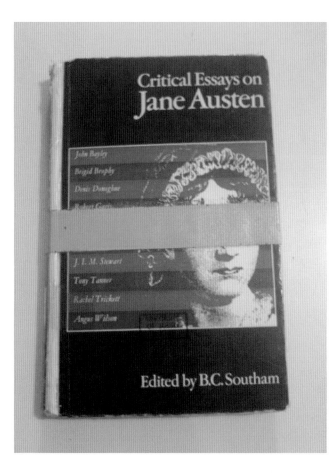

World's Best Accidental Transition Into Punk.

World's Best Double Life.

World's Best Options.

World's Least Appetising Snack.

World's Least Appropriate Font.

World's Least Reassuring Sign.

World's Most Aspirational Tinned Goods.

World's Most Chauvinistic Dog.

World's Most Hardcore Teddy.

World's Greatest Battle.

World's Most Transparent Attempt To Inject Some
Much Needed Glamour Into The World Of Maths.

World's Most Lootable Shop.

World's Most Optimistic Shoe.

World's Most Loveable Vandalism.

World's Most Humiliating Endorsement.

World's Worst Secret Millionaire.

World's Freakiest Children's Party.

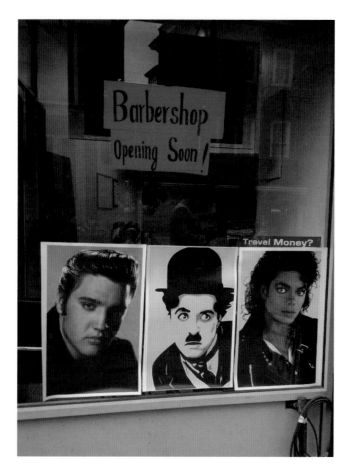

World's Worst Options.

World's Best Home Security System.

World's Most Niche Bachelor Foodstuff.

World's Most Traumatic Pudding.

World's Hardest Bastard.

World's Best Subgenre.

World's Bluntest Message To Paedophiles.

World's Worst Bunting.

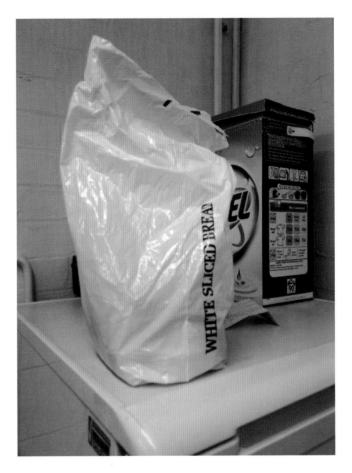

World's Least Fancy Bread.

World's Bleakest Cake.

World's Most Apparently Useless Sign.

World's Most Basic Tree.

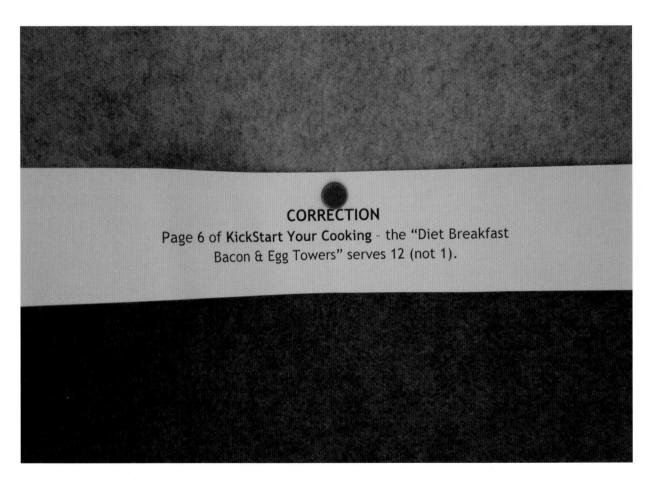

CORRECTION

Page 6 of **KickStart Your Cooking** - the "Diet Breakfast Bacon & Egg Towers" serves 12 (not 1).

World's Most Consequential Typo.

World's Least Appropriate Children's Protagonist.

World's Least Feminine Toiletry.

World's Least Cool Tag.

World's Most Immature Use Of A Cameraphone.

World's Most Immature Use Of A Cameraphone.

World's Most Fortified Nothing.

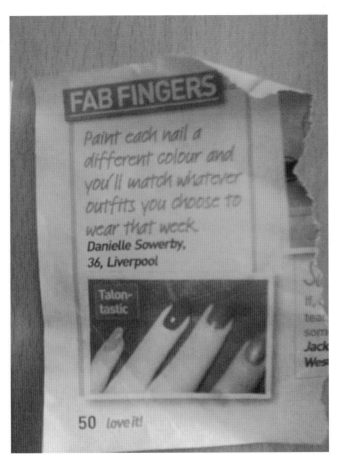

World's Most Fundamentally Flawed Tip.

World's Most Suspicious Shop.

World's Most Historical Purveyor Of Erotica.

World's Most Confusingly Named Deodorant Brand.

World's Most Enigmatic Condiment.

World's Most Confusing Bales Of Hay.

World's Drunkest Cupboard.

World's Most Badass Gran.

Desserts

174 Vietnamese Rainbow Drink   2.50
(Mung Beans, Gelatinous Seaweed and Coconut Milk)
Chè ba màu

175 Fresh Soya Milk(Warm or Cold)   2.20
Sữa đậu nành (nóng và lạnh)

Coffee & Tea

World's Worst Dessert Menu.

World's Worst Babysitters.

World's Best Priorities.

World's Most Amusingly Phallic Sign.

World's Most Potent Nerd Aphrodisiac.

World's Worst Autumn Look.

World's Least Expertly Applied Fake Tan.

World's Most Perverse Commuter.

World's Most Intolerant Car.

World's Most Arrogant Album.

World's Most Significantly Empty Chairs.

World's Sneakiest Mannequin.

World's Least Reassuring Doctors Surgery.

World's Grittiest Dollhouse.

World's Most Terrifying Company Mascot.

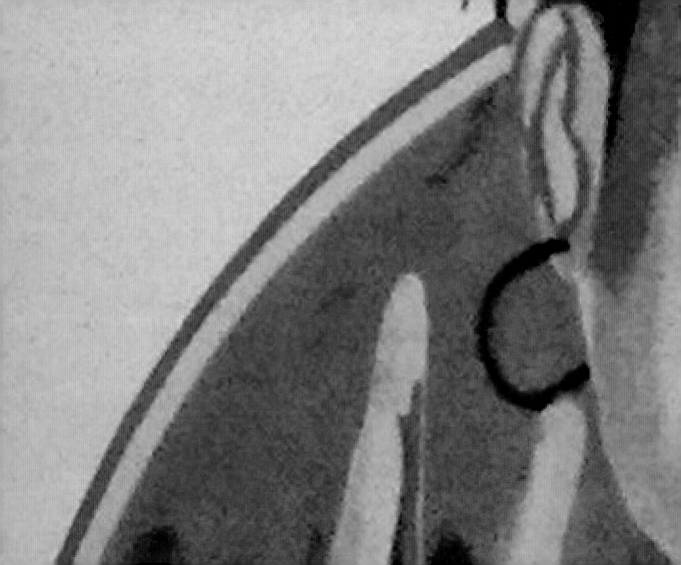

World's Greatest Fall From Grace.

World's Most Upbeat Undertakers.

GREAT PRICE

Mr Kipling Mice Pies
6 Pack

£1.50

World's Most Nightmarish Christmas.

World's Most Highly Pressurised Scenario For The Obese.

World's Most Catastrophically Poor Choice Of Book Giveaway
By The Red Cross When Afforded The Power Of Hindsight.

World's Most Impressive Nap.

No Caption Required.

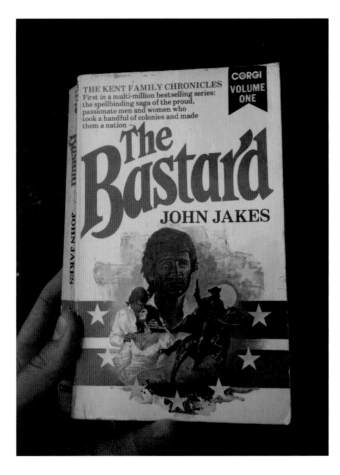

World's Least Subtle Characterisation.

World's Most Eligible Bachelors.

World's Most Segregated Biscuits.

World's Greatest Proof That Children Are Psychopaths.

World's Most Laughable Suggestion.

World's Nosiest Poster,
And That Doesn't
Even Take Into Account Its
Rather Unfortunately Named
Campaign Representative.

World's Least Successful Attempt At An Individual Look.

World's Greatest Proof That Paedophiles Are Trying To
Corrupt Our Children By Any Means Necessary.

World's Least Troubled Dog.

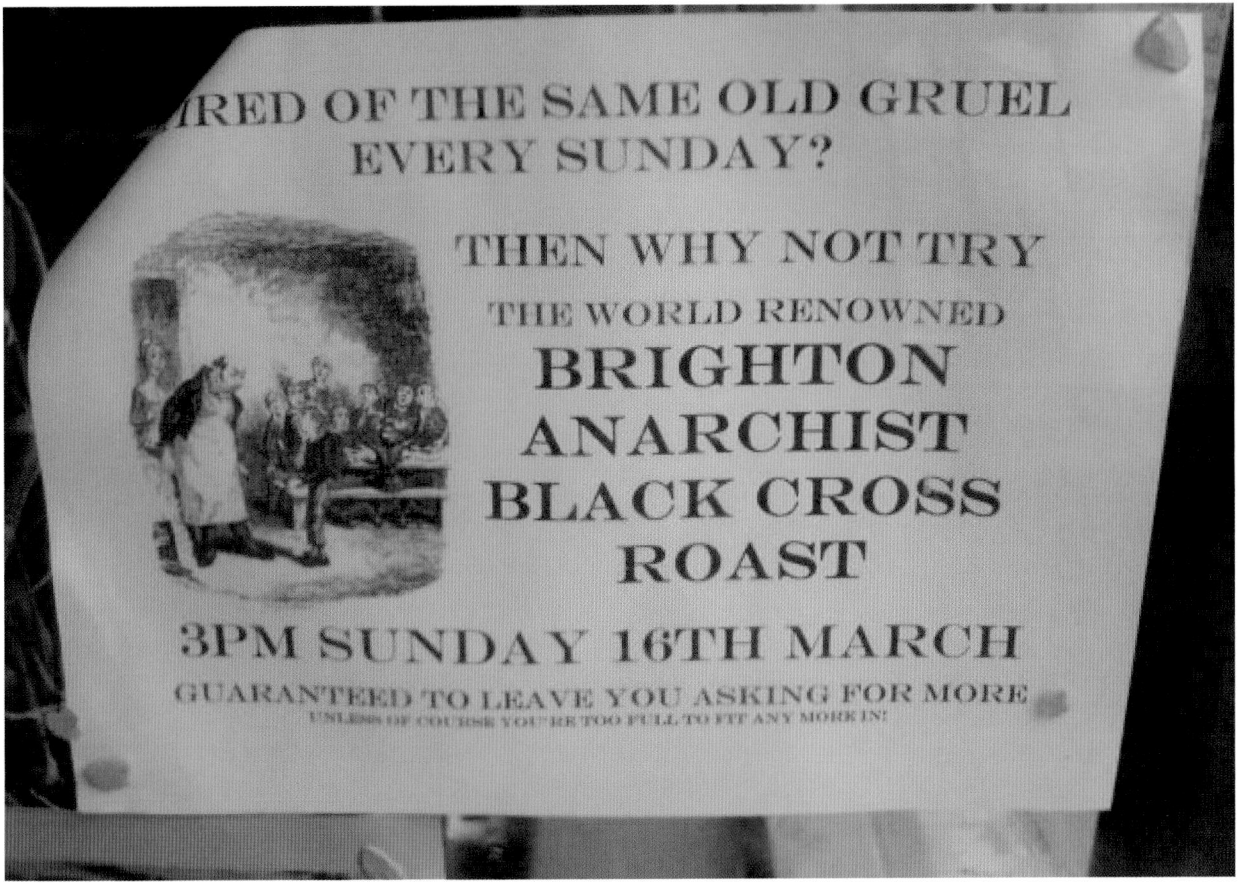

World's Most Adorable Anarchists.

World's Most Doomed Meal For Two.

World's Most Pessimistic Back-To-School Stationery.

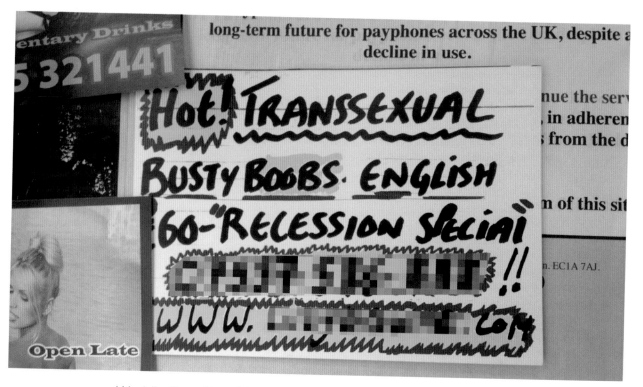

World's Best Use Of A Global Economic Downturn For Profit.